What the Mouth Was Made For

Katherine Riegel

FUTURECYCLE PRESS

Mineral Bluff, Georgia

Published by FutureCycle Press
Mineral Bluff, Georgia, USA

ISBN 978-1-938853-04-3

Contents

because of love

I

For poetry makes nothing happen: it survives
In the valley of its making where executives
Would never want to tamper, flows on south
From ranches of isolation and the busy griefs,
Raw towns that we believe and die in; it survives,
A way of happening, a mouth.

—W. H. Auden, from "In Memory of W. B. Yeats"

Describing Green to My Colorblind Friend

Smell of alfalfa, texture
of polished wood, and water, and the crook
of your elbow. Green is both dark
and daytime, new hardcover books and footraces
across the sand to dive into the sea. Green tastes like mint
and hay and joy. I wish

I could explain it better. Imagine
this: you wake up one night
when the moon is very high
and the ceiling is made of leaves.
You sit up and fly
from branch to branch. Every
perch in the canopy of trees
gives you a different view of the moon.
It looks like the marble
you secretly put in your mouth and held
on your tongue when you were five. As you
move you see it is spilled wax, an opening
fist, a dolphin's back, a fingerprint, a clover;
it is a mirror, and it shows

your bird self, perfectly ready
to sing yourself back to sleep and
dream of the wild places of the earth
lifting their faces to be kissed.

The Swallowing

With the twirl of my tongue I encompass worlds and volumes of worlds.

—*Walt Whitman, from "Song of Myself"*

Sadness crouches
deep down in my throat where it opens
onto memory, where possibilities flutter
their crooked wings and large-eyed mammals
spin light from the stars. I do not even know
what I want from the world but
this: night, wind, movement, a delicate prickling
on my skin like the clutching feet of insects,
circles in the earth, music like a map,
life in all its myriad and alien
forms rushing at me,
in me, a great swallowing.

The Sangamon River

First came the rains, and then the druids
and their trees. They sang ancient songs built
of prairie grass and mud; they sang

great four-winged birds sweeping
over the land; they sang crickets and low-
down summer afternoons;

they sang the possibilities of fire
and the echoes of green,
sweet flat fields and bubbly

little hills. They sang heralds
and myths, slinking beasts and rolling beasts,
leaf-vein and frog-skin and horse-breath;

they sang dank and cold; they sang gold
and juniper and Osage orange.
The river rose up its serpent head,

hissed out deer and raccoon and fox,
lay down with the catfish and crawdads
to dream under the tired trees.

Some time later, I came to live there, and the river
curled at my side like innocent rope
I could never stop twining through my fingers.

I Wish to Be (But Am Not) a Bodhisattva

When love rushes in like the sea
and undermines the sand beneath me, I want

to reach into that person's body
and cradle whatever I find there:

tree with three birds living in it,
purple grass growing all the way down

to the edge of the stream, bulging
frog singing lost ancient songs,

mountain meadow with sage hanging from its mouth
like a horse delirious in a field of alfalfa. I want

kingdoms of clover for us to lie in, crushing
the sweet white blooms, and crowns

made of raspberries and bees
circling our heads like prophets;

and I want my shifty marble-filled shadow
to sidle up to his and something

like arms to shape themselves from longing
and blood so we can touch each other

in the places that cry out their need
like mice too young to open their eyes

or to know whatever is knowable in this
nearly uninhabitable world.

The Lost Birds

(imperial woodpecker, ivory-billed woodpecker, passenger pigeon, Eskimo curlew, great auk, Carolina parakeet, Labrador duck...)

1. wing through the otherworld, waiting
for us. They follow our running selves,
picking up the thorns and rags we leave
behind, and they sew
new bodies for us all. In the next world of color,
we may wake up
with feathers.

2. They do not know
they are lost, though everyone believes
in the lost birds now that they are
gone.

3. Sometimes, we think
we catch the lost birds
in our periphery and we know
they are beads of water
on a string, hollow gourds
that sing only when they are
together.

4. At night, the lost
birds blink and when they open
their eyes we see out of them
and try, once again, to fly.

Chimes

We rescue tiny frogs from our swimming pool,
jewels of gold and green the size
of a freckle or
half my pinky fingernail, their bodies
guileless, the splayed toes with their suction-cup
endings, the black eyes as wise as a whale's.
We scoop them out of the chlorinated water
and deposit them in the potted bromeliads, hoping
the soupy ponds of the centers are
what they need to live, imagining
them diving there like mermaids in a seaweed jungle
eating mosquito larvae and whatever
troubles the edges of those pink serrated leaves;

or sometimes, thinking of overcrowded
high-rises, we curl
our hands and ferry
them outside to the birdbath and its
dangerous open water.

We don't know what happens
to them, so many
predators out there and thousands
of leaves to hide under; we don't know
where they breed or if they ever
grow bigger; we know only they carry

something more delicate and powerful than watch gears
inside their glistening skins;
and when the winter comes we will speak of them,

saying the names we have
thought to give them: little golden bell, orb of summer, breath
of rain, whisper disappearing
into the grass.

The Uncertainty Principle

The lights blink out across this state
and the river animals don't speak to us
when we bend down and our hair
touches the water's surface. The last
mystery is the dark inside
our heads, inside the bones
of our knees. No wonder
we cannot understand each other,
half our words so obvious
they don't need saying and the other half
missing—

The sea rushes to fill us.
Sand arranges itself like galaxies.
I don't know if you define *hope*
the way I do. I don't know how to ask you.
Sometimes I pretend the seagulls are flying
into a world much quieter than this one, somewhere
I might want to live.
I know what they are crying
as they fly away from me, wings
cupping the air like a beloved face:
We are lonely. We are lonely. We are lonely.

II

That hard nugget of pain, I would suck it,
cradling it on my tongue like the slick
seed of pomegranate. I would lift it

tenderly, as a great animal might
carry a small one in the private
cave of the mouth.

—*Ellen Bass, from "Basket of Figs"*

What I'm Afraid Of

Being tied down, pushed
down, held down, and hurt with
burning tools, human appendages,
knives. Being
sliced like a pot roast. Watching
an alligator eat my dog. Hitting
a raccoon with my car. Losing my
memory and my mind, weighing down
those I love, the smell of chemicals overtaking
the air, being buried, failing
to keep everyone safe. Coughs that flower
with blood. Irrational
people. Becoming lost
in a city. Trying
so hard I make myself a fool; not
trying hard enough. June bugs,
but not spiders or snakes. Early
mornings, sometimes. Aging
poorly, broken hips, surgeries, smelly
bags attached with indignity.
Not having the chance
to end it myself before it all
goes to shit. Not knowing
joy when I see it. Forgetting
what I'm not afraid of, remembering
only the pain.

Something I Was Meant to Know

Signs are broken flowers,
the boy says, and the words
circle the truck like sparks searching
for a way out. So many broken
lit-up flowers out tonight:
lining this strip-malled street,
exploding (still) over our heads
because it is the 4th of July until midnight
at least. Nothing

changes. Children scream at the detonations
like they did on the Bicentennial,
the year my mother said
cotton candy was just air and sugar,
so I spent my coins on good solid chocolate instead,
and we watched fireflies talking back to the lights overhead
from their secret places in the grass.
Someone tries to hand me a sparkler and I back away;
I've never trusted burning things. Tears,

for instance. Or spicy peppers, stars, desire.
All of these can blow out
your insides like a house fire,
leaving a charred skeleton slumped
by the roadside. Gods of the prairie sky,
teach me how to eat the torn petals
of these flowers you keep dropping in my path.

Thirst

Perhaps because they are so
sweet, so many
tropical plants have teeth. Isn't that
always the way? The liquid pulp inside
suitable to slake any
animal thirst, but the only way
to get to it is through pain.
Protect, protect, protect
the thorns sing, always ready to bite,
and we are the plush heart
inside the cage. But we also
hunger, we also thirst.
So we reach out to
touch leaves, stem, fruit;
we carry water
from mouth to mouth; we tend
what must be tended—green lives
full of secrets—giving
our little offerings of blood
because what's inside this garden
is just what we need.

Feeding Time

Let's feed tears to the dragons
of misery, but let's never crawl into their mouths.

—Cristin O'Keefe Aptowicz,
from "Op-Ed for the Sad Sack Review,
Regarding News of Another Rash of Writer Suicides"

Because dragons
have to live, too. I heard they get off
on our despair like the devil
is supposed to. I just
don't want to glow with pathos
like someone with a black hole stuck
to the bottom of her shoe who keeps
wondering why the world is half-
disappearing behind her. Or, worse,
doesn't, because she never looks back
to see the terrifying jagged edge of nothing
like a glossy magazine photo torn
down the middle.

        And if you think
I'm exaggerating, if you bring up
leaves like sequins in the waterlight
or Devonshire cream or clean sheets,
you'll force me to use the kind of language
no one should have to hear—blood and running
and yelps and brokenness—and then try
to explain about the outlet malls
we wander in a constant tension of desire
to possess beauty
and fear that we never will,

certain that no matter how long we take
we will make the wrong decision and end up
paying more than we can afford.

                    Really
we should thank those dragons
with their cat-rough tongues that hurt
just right against our seared skin
and their lips as red as kisses
and those teeth that look like bridges
to some better place but lock
almost every time against us
for our own miserable good.

Years Like Rows of Corn

1. I wanted to live
on light, to drink
from streams glowing
the green-gold of fireflies.
I read too much. I believed
everything we should tell children
not to believe.

2. I stood close to the burn barrel
where we lit our trash
on fire and the heat snipped away
a little of my hair, just the strands
along my right temple. I fell
back and the static sound
stopped and I smelled
my own luck.

3. Other things
I believed: that I would not fall
when I climbed in the barn rafters;
that finding four-leafed clovers
in the backyard and pressing them
between soft pages would preserve
that place forever; that all animals
would listen to me
like our horses did, puffing
sweet breath from their nostrils,
lowering their heads to mine.

4. Water, too, had its chance
at me, the floodwaters of the Sangamon
carrying me over the drainage ditch
so my feet touched only
snake-like weeds that twined
around my ankles—
the same waters that kept the dark loam
of our lower pasture fertile
so the horses grew fat
on agile grasses.

5. Again and again, I open
the door on what I lost:
small farm above the river
on a blacktop road meant
for bikes in summer and sleds
in winter. Huge breathing sky,
red tulips in the bend of the driveway.

6. My blood
balloons in my veins; I float
over years like rows of corn.
I lean over myself at ten. I don't
know if I want to give
that child some warning or take
her in my arms and run
off into the fields
where at least
we do not have to fear
because we have nothing
left that can be stolen.

Hide and Seek

What do we translate, sitting in our closets
alone, coats swaying over our heads, rough tweed
hems mussing our hair, too
tall now but somehow still children
playing hide and seek in small spaces, always?

>   Questions written by the veins
>   in your arms; unfenced memory.

Do we need permission to talk
to the dead?

>   No; but to talk to the living
>   whose nearness you can't gauge
>   you must bring an offering
>   of white feathers.

Was it easier
in the caves, in the mountains, in the cornfields,
by the sea, before the electric
eels we step amongst now, before we knew
we were?

>   Tell your pain. Tell knives
>   raining from the sky, running impossible
>   distances. Tell lifting the cup to drink
>   and your throat gone missing. Tell cracks
>   scissoring through the ground. Tell, because the language
>   of things is the hardest story
>   you know. Tell because someone
>   needs you, heart laid against his heart
>   like a pair of shadow puppets in the dark.

Even in the Pretend World (There Is Longing)

There's a small man in the machine
in the Exact Change Only lane at the toll stop,
counting the coins as they slide
through the opening. He's got a hacking
cough, the kind that starts in the lungs
and bursts up through the windpipe
and carries a little of the throat away with it.
He grumbles when some careless motorist
tosses in a Canadian dime instead of a nickel.

Expect an uprising any day now,
a real Marxist revolution, millions
of little grit-faced workers, tired
of the darkness and the cramped space,
dissatisfied with the river of silver
that used to cool their fevered hearts.
After all, there must be better jobs—
decorating dollhouses, repairing music boxes,
holding the palette for an artist
and staring at the model
hour after hour, eyes fixed on beauty—
or plainness, it wouldn't matter—
as long as there was light
reflecting off the dust, prismed in the window.

I'm Not One of You

I open my appropriate mouth...

—*Jericho Brown, from "Lunch"*

My inappropriate mouth
speaks from tree trunks, bathroom mirrors, and the rubber
soles of shoes. It opens too wide
and frightens the neighbors. It is lined
with inappropriate teeth, sharp as porcupine quills and capable
of pipe organ music. It chews gum
and library books, holds long conversations
with Japanese beetles. *Too many*
people walk the beaten sidewalks,
it says. *Criminals*
should be fed air and maintained
every 3000 miles. Don't rule out
a revenge of the dandelions. Nobody
knows what it's talking about. The man in the airplane
next to me says how much the Haitians
hate white people in Miami and
my inappropriate mouth tries to open
between my clenched knees, tries to say *What's not*
to hate? It is full
of clever comebacks and the kind of dizzy
bullshit people hate to love. It slavers
and spits, biting into the back of strangers'
necks. I am afraid
of what it will do next. If it gets loose,
it will run through the neighborhood shouting
I'm not one of you until
it has incited all the houses and mailboxes

to sit up and unfurl
their bloody grins and tell us what
they really think.

The Dreams

The one where you have to scream and no sound comes out, nothing at all, not even the sucking sound that happens when the drain suddenly unclogs and the water runs to its next life in the sewers...

The one where you need to call the fire department or the police or ambulance and your phone is broken, taken over by some virus you can't stop that makes little dragons out of x's and o's that fly around your screen in endless circles...

The one where you're sent back to high school, trying to swim through the hallways filled with the thick, viscous weight of your adolescence and all its disappointments...

The one where you open the door to the backyard and there are dozens of dogs instead of just your three and some of them are the dead dogs you loved and had to put into the hands of the vet saying *Please...*

The one where your parents are saying *okay* and signing some mysterious document when you walk in and they don't even try to hide it because they think you will approve but you know it's wrong, wrong, monstrously and horribly wrong, they are selling you into shame...

The one where you're driving and get lost and find yourself on sidewalks and alleys and people's backyards afraid the cops will come after you afraid of who you might hurt and then there's a narrow bridge and if you pull the wheel just wrong you will go toppling over the side...

The one where you're singing in some choir but you can't remember the words and you're dressed all wrong and your solo is coming up but you have no idea what the melody even sounds like...

The one where you're moving but have to collect your stuff from multiple places and when you go with a box and a backpack you find too much to fit into such measly offerings: old furniture and jewelry from your mother's mother and giant bookshelves you'd love to have but could not fit in any size house you might ever live in...

The one where you're dying to have sex my god it's been so long and you find your lover (husband sometimes ex-boyfriend sometimes stranger with familiar eyes) and kiss and make your way to a room and close the door only to find people looking in the window or calling for you expecting an answer people who will come in without knocking and you wake up aching...

Fields

were stillness and weight; childhood
was an outfit we only got to wear once;
softness was fur and the warm
breathing under it, and a river

was a little silver necklace strung
with emeralds and mud.
A sledding hill was a hot tar road in July and a
memory of birth later on. Landscape
carried a symphony and a scale
to measure everything we wanted:

cornfields understood us and soybeans
understood the sky and alfalfa
smelled like horse breath
and nobody should have tasted the rusty fence
but we did

and what we called Indian summer
was all gold light like ginger ale
and only really big trees
were quiet enough

and anything
thrown high into the air
was a song, a mystery, a beat
or two of happiness—

if you ask me
what it was like
growing up there

I could tell you
about all the languages I knew but
other than green the most important
one was silence.

Portents

I was supposed to be a bird
in this life,
not some ragged
animal falling backwards into a green pool—

∞

Hail, that hard dream
in the lost book of a summer thunderstorm.
A great sigh of collective voices.
Nothing to see
until a flash—

∞

Where the whispers of fire and night air?
The rushing of a terrible nature,
the beauty of fangs everywhere?
How can loneliness stretch and stretch into a million
breakings
and still be one great stony keep?

∞

The tree with the door in its trunk—

∞

Once I was so young even the dew
knew more from the moments
it witnessed, goodbyes and clutched
hellos in the semi-dark.

∞

You surrender—
a white handkerchief in my driveway—

∞

I am thinking of a seam
running down the middle of my chest
that I might rip open
to save us.

What I'd Like to Find at the Bottom of My Cereal Box

A white pelican, and a lake for her to float on, and a tiny island in the middle of the lake where she will raise little clouds every year

A game of tag like we used to play in the arena, on horseback, dirt rising into the air like butterfly scales while the horses ducked and turned on their haunches

A swatch of fabric so perfectly magenta that it could not be any other color and so defines the essence of magenta the way Tyrone Power defines the essence of black and white film idol

A treasure map with curving dotted lines I can follow to get to the one spot unmarked by confusion

An ornate fan inlaid with gold and silver and the faint tracery of caramelized tears so when it is opened the world begins, glittering, to cry

III

He says fire is the basis for all forms of the mouth.

—Bob Hicok, from "In Michael Robins's class minus one"

Boys

And this: kissing a boy
in a hayloft while my friend
waited just outside the hay bale fort
for her turn. Not enough
boys to go around in our neighborhood, I guess, or at least
no others with those bright brown eyes looking
out at the world with enough curiosity and desire
to tractor us both in
as if we might find pieces of ourselves
that had gone missing in our previous lives. I buried
my nose in his t-shirt just above the clavicle
and inhaled the perfume of my future
obsession, how I would always want
the perfect boy to smell: like late summer
and horses and clover; like dry
Illinois dirt and thunderstorms, tree
swings, garter snakes, sticks held like rifles
at the shoulder, overgrown
zucchini all the neighbors were
always trying to give away, snap beans
and penny bubble gum and hard well-water;
like the ghost of his grandfather
saving that boy from a house fire; like my mother
waking up one more time safe
after a seizure;
like names written on the underside
of a one-lane bridge; like blacktop
and good dark mud and orange clouds;
like breath orbiting a dust-smeared face
as sweet as dried alfalfa.

Need: A Sestina

for Mike Capel

You love wistful paintings of boys
leaning on each other, not talking,
something more than companionship and less than desire
between them, nearly as soothing and addictive as smoke.
You try to name what you see in words
strong and simple enough there is no getting lost

in the streets of an unfamiliar city, despite lost
bikes, mothers, music, rings. Boys
fight, and steal, and you struggle with words
that sometimes make you lonely, though talking
and cigarettes help, because smoking
allows you to be both inside and outside the scene. Your desire

for the world of men and their unnamable desires
leads you into nights ringing with celebration and loss,
making noise with everything you've got, even the smell of smoke
loud on your clothes and in your hair. In your stories I can see the boy
you were, I can hear you talking
to him and all his tragic friends, using words

even he might recognize as incantations. Did you know then words
would be both the object of and the gateway to your desire?
You must have always listened to people talking,
noting the tidal movements of conversations, the way lost
wavelets of meaning lap belatedly at the shore, to give your boys
such perfect, nearly careless things to say. Sometimes when you smoke

you invite me, too, telling me I need to take up smoking
for the conversation, the peculiar dream of words
that comes when a couple of boys
stand around on a concrete stoop under the sky and desire
shrinks to the size of a match and a red ember. What is loss
then but ash falling away? And there is always talk

to take its place. Did I say I love your talk
with all its currents and swift-moving slivers of smoke?
I know something about loss
myself, about the sweetness and betrayal of words
written and spoken, or neither, about the desire
to lie down and seal that place inside. I know you are not a boy

anymore, despite my talk, and I hope you will forgive my words
meant as some kind of smoky solace for us both. What you desire
is your own to find or lose, not-boy painting your life on the page.

White Heath, Illinois

—after Jeffrey McDaniel's "Origins"

I'm from softball in the backyard and bubbling tar roads.

I'm from 6 a.m. trudges through snow to the barn to feed the horses and breaking ice out of water buckets in the predawn dark.

I'm from loading up the manure spreader and watching its wicked spikes toss the manure across the pasture in arcs of flying shit.

I'm from electric fences and driveways covered in fist-sized gravel.

I'm from a half-hour drive to the nearest hospital.

I'm from *we don't say ain't and keep your elbows off the table or I'll stab them with a fork.*

I'm from built-in bookshelves rising to the ceiling.

I'm from well-water so hard and full of flavor you could chew it.

I'm from melting icicles in the gas stove because the power out means the water pump doesn't work.

I'm from barn rafters and hay forts, dirt clod fights and running from the neighbor's pack of dogs.

I'm from a grandfather without a high school education and one who was a prosecuting lawyer in the courtroom when Al Capone got sent away for tax evasion.

I'm from folk music and singing in the station wagon.

I'm from *stop giggling back there or I'll tie you on the top of the car and prop your mouth open to catch flies.*

I'm from cowering at the dinner table while my father roars like a wild boar speared from the inside.

I'm from so many miles of sky you can't count.

The Siren Song of Corn Country

Come down to the sea
my love, to the dirt-deep prairie waters,
the cold rush of high water levels,
the sure devouring of wind.

I want to ask you
and the earthworms
if life underneath is sweeter
than above.

I would be a swimmer
in the lush soil, a maker of patterns
in snow-foam.

There are secrets down here,
pyrite and quartz,
taste of clover-seed and moss-spore,
the glacial movements of bedrock.

At first
you will squeeze shut your eyes
and hold your breath,

but soon the heaviness will begin to shine
smooth as dolphin-skin,
and I promise
you will not miss the air.

Changeling

Growing up in the cornfields, I believed in other worlds
reached through mirrors or secret doors or dark openings in trees.
I disappeared into books so completely I became invisible,
a quiet child gone so quiet I left only an indentation on the pillow
and looked out from behind the printed words like an animal
peering furtively from the thorny underbrush. No fairies

ever came to steal me away, replace me with a fairy
child, changeling, animated block of wood and mud. In the world
I wanted, *what is* became *what might be,* animals
might lend you their speed or flight, trees
sang to the stars with leaves as bright as fireflies, my pillow
floated over our house, and invisible

feathered beings played with moonlight while I slept, invisible
above the tangle of my family. I knew perfectly well fairies
were not to be trusted, capricious and inconsistent as a strange pillow.
Still I thought I would understand a world
where what I had to worry about most was which tree
sheltered the wrong kind of toadstool or what animal

I could trust to tell me the way to the nearest animal's
village better than I fathomed the invisible
trip wires of my father's rage. When I could, I went into the trees,
crawling under the grapevines so I could look for fairies
where I had the best chance of finding them. There are worlds
we return to night after night, tireless, the pillow

itself a doorway. There are hard asphalt dreams no pillow
can soften. I have had enough of these, the tender animal
inside curled on itself so tightly no clever words

will coax or soothe it. I am carrying an invisible
girl through the streets. We are looking for fairies.
We are looking for the sky. We are looking for trees

tall enough to be pillars in a great hall, trees
tended by graceful dryads. We renounce sleep and pillows.
We examine the faces of all we meet for a trace of fairy
blood. We carry four-leaf clovers. We know what animal
we would be in another life: a swift cheetah or an invisible
bird. We know there are keys to the otherworld

made of words. In the shadows of the trees, animals
dance. Under our pillows we find treasures that turn invisible
in our fingers. Fairies watch us slyly, waiting, across the worlds.

Sam Never Uses the Word Love

Your answer to any question
takes time. *Uhhhh,* you say, drawing
it out like a negotiator stalling
to trace the kidnapper's call.
Even when casual, your clothes
fit without sag or wrinkle.
You are methodical
with a menu. Conversation is serious
unless you're teasing me about my
age. Youngster, you have no
knowledge of suffering. You
are beloved, lucky, effortlessly
beautiful, good. You don't sit
on the floor of your office, rocking,
wondering what poison you served
in a previous life that eats your heart
in tiny vicious bites now. You don't know
lonely. You don't know empty. But

then you look across the table
with your cloud eyes and say,
I lost her. You do not want
another dog, and I finally
understand; and I wish I could
tell you grief is no reason
not to love, I wish I could bring back
all our loves, I wish the world
would prove its love to us both every
fucking day. My friend, you are the only
self you have. Tonight, dream
of fur under your fingertips.

Tonight, climb out of that boat
carrying you untouched down the river
and splash across to the sharp grass
of the shore. Reach for that dangerous
fruit, messy and addictive and ephemeral
as a sigh.

Ten Weeks In

1. My father
shakes and whimpers, his worry gathered
into corporeality and standing guard
over him. Its hot feline breath
fogs his glasses; he cannot see or
taste or remember his own birthday...

I carry this image around
to the grocery store, the library, the inside
of my own house. I talk on the phone, say
chemical imbalance, breakdown.
It is like swallowing
stones.

2. These belong to my father and me: dreams
of driving out of control, him in the back seat in his
and my feet not reaching the pedals in mine. Green
eyes. Unerasable images of what could go wrong—knives
falling from the counter onto innocent canine heads,
crashes of all varieties, heirloom furniture scratched
by the movers, a pulled thread unraveling
until there is nothing left.

3. In the dark behind me,
there is a rustling.
I will not
turn around.

Four Nights After My Father Died,

I dreamed I was going to his funeral, but
I had spent the day with the dogs and horses and I was
sweaty, dusty, wearing jeans and a t-shirt and muddy
boots. I had no time to go home and shower
and change into appropriate
clothes—something dark, a dress even, and
panty hose in narrow shoes. I was
panicking, the feeling rising into my throat
like tears, as I entered the dim church
with its polished walnut pews, a church
like the one my father went to as a child
but taller, stainedglass windows nearly
infinite up to a lit ceiling. Then
I saw my father, sitting quietly
near the back, wearing a casual
navy blue suit and smiling. No one
else saw him. He patted the seat
next to him, glowing
with comfort. "Why don't you
sit here with me?" he said, and took
my hand. "I bet this will be nice."
And then I knew
my father was happier than he had been—in life
he would have glared at my played-in clothes—
so I sat down, and the music bubbled
around our feet like the sea,
and my father smiled while it kept rising
and rising.

Belief

Come away, O human child!
To the waters and the wild
With a faery, hand in hand,
For the world's more full of weeping than you can
understand.

—W. B. Yeats, from "The Stolen Child"

Tonight the dark outside is an ongoing cry
of grief, no longer sharp, something like a siren in the mouth
of a cave. I'm missing
crawling on elbows and knees under the wild roses,
down the slope to the big tree
that swallowed all the secrets I offered it
through the t-shirt I wore when I leaned
my summer-sweat back against its bark.

Tonight water is collecting
in the hollows of great stone monuments under the sky
like the ones I dreamt
in the cornfields of Illinois
to house the mysteries I sensed
in the ancient dirt of that place,
palace of all my green memories.

Tonight I will bring together
honeysuckle and ash, river-trace and my whole
collection of feathers,
and I will chant *October October October*—
month of swelling nights and opening
doors—until the dark rises up and comes
to meet me and looks into the wild raw spaces in my eyes
and says my name.

IV

Make in your mouths the words that were our names

—Archibald MacLeish,
from "Epistle to be Left in the Earth"

Hydra

What's neat is I can see me with all my heads!

—*Charlotte Alessio Manier,*
4 years old, on looking at her reflection
in the back of a silver pinwheel

1. This head sits by the window, watching others in the frenetic clasp of fun, envious, sun-starved, growing.

2. Gold adorns this head like a blossom.

3. This head sings songs of torment from the bottom of the sea.

4. This head has a tongue of stone.

5. *To tie a headstrong girle from love, is to tie the Furies again in fetters.*

6. After cutting off Medusa's head, Perseus lifted it by its snaky hair.

7. This head imagines a late summer day: drifting dragonflies, the shade of a gnarled tree, the taste of apples.

8. This head makes a shadow on the sidewalk. It opens its mouth, and the concrete speaks.

9. This is the head of a girl aflame in a world waiting for combustion.

I Dream My Mother

They say when you dream a horse
that horse is your spirit.

—Judith Barrington, from "Horses and the Human Soul"

I dream my mother is a gardenia.
I dream my mother alive
still, her funeral
a fake, and she gradually recovering muscle,
mind, color and breath for the past three years
in Connecticut, where I would never
have thought to look for her.
I dream my mother as
Ophelia, drifting down the clear river,
singing. I dream my mother
a horse so she can ride across my backyard, leaving
hoof prints in the flowerbeds. I dream my
mother in feathers, flippers, fur. I dream
my mother in the morning, coffee mug in her hand, dust
in the pale light. I dream her carrying
a coffee can full of grain and whistling
in the barn. I dream her asking
questions of the air, and the air
answering. I dream her afraid; I dream her telling me
not to be afraid. I dream her on the phone,
inside an envelope, in riding boots, in tears.
I dream her asleep and I dream her waking
and, opening
                my eyes to the mirror,
I see—what?—an apology
of lashes, a seed in the iris that will take years
to bloom.

Jacqueline and the Beanstalk

What if it was
a girl who traded the family cow
for a handful of magic that just might
save her from domestic
dullness, a girl who
bowed her head in despair when her mother
threw the beans out the window and mentioned
in the same moment that the butcher's
son was looking for a wife and don't
roll your eyes like that because how else
do you expect us to live now?
And what if Jacqueline (she never
liked Jackie) saw that beanstalk the next
morning and climbed it instead
of making the first pot of coffee, lured
by the great big smell
of possibility?

No, maybe the story wouldn't
have turned out the same.
What would you do
in some other world held up
by green, looking down at all you knew
as from a great balcony,
something rich and frightening and larger
than dreams on its way
to overtake you?

Some River

On the bank of some river she waits,
irresolute, near tears, hands around the sharp stick
of her fear, while the other horses slip
happily into the dark water
and her mother and sister encourage her to come
in. Her horse is hot, she is hot, but she has seen horses roll

at the smell of mud and she can feel herself rolling
under the surface, the others waiting
too long for her to reappear before they come
down to get her, her feet stuck
in the stirrups, the water
filling her riding hat while she slips

away forever. It's no use telling her she will live, her horse is a ship
that will not capsize with her on top. She will roll
her eyes like some wild thing; she does not trust water
and never will. She will wait
on the bank, rigid in her unhappiness, stuck.
Eventually the others will come

back, and they will not ask her to come
into the river again. She has her reasons to slip
away from that confrontation: once, a horse stuck
in the deep mud had to be pulled out by tractor, the giant tires rolling
heavily across leaves and roots while the horse waited
to get his footing and scramble desperately out of the water.

Once she went down to play in the water
lapping the blacktop after a flood. Tall weeds came
curling around her legs and though she whispered *wait*

it did not take the current long to slip
her far from the shallows. Helpless fatigue rolled
through her while she stuck

her chin as high as it would go—her breath sticking
in her throat like water—
until at last her voice rolled
far enough along the surface and her mother came
striding out in her clothes.
                              Don't say these things slip
into memory, fade, and are gone. That girl I was knows they wait

for you to forget, stick your foot in too far, and then come
rushing up to claim you, pull you into the water and slip
their wet fingers into your hair, roll you forever in a blanket of silt.

Manifesto

Housework is a darkness behind the eyes,
two friends fighting in front of you, colonies
of ants, a recent humiliation by someone
much younger. Every dirty dish turns pestilence
when it's time for washing. The whole thing
is a Sisyphean task. How many years
do we sleep, again? Twenty-five to thirty, if we're lucky?
I don't want to give any of my years to housework
or to arguing about it, the femi-nazi me (as
my students like to say) unable to do one minute more
than anyone else in the house.
Let me garden, mow, paint, fix. Let laundry
do itself. Let food appear in little boxes.
Let dust transform into miniature cleaning robots,
polish everything. After I die
let me come back centuries from now, to that perfect
sci-fi world, or else back
to some kind of beginning, when woman looked at the leaves
on the floor and thought simply
How beautiful.

The Garden to Which We Return

I am looking in the azaleas
for my mother, born in late March—season
of green and fresh storms. But the grove

of longleaf pines smells like her, and the ferns
are the curls at her neck after a ride
on her big chestnut gelding. Perhaps

she is crouching among the bromeliads
and thinking of her mother's sharp
tongue. Or chasing a dragonfly

through the bamboo like the child
she always remained, her ghost-shadow
teaching her how to slip

between tattooed stalks. I know
she is here, though the fields we shared
are miles and years away. I know she sings

in this riotous garden, because my heart
beats like wings and the incense of gardenia
hovers over me like a promise.

Creation

In a forest on the edge
of the world a woman
reaches into her chest,
fingers pushing through
layers of muscle and fat,
breast and ribcage. She
withdraws a splinter
and holds it between her fingers,
then buries it in the fragrant
leaf mold under the hanging
universe of green. She will

miss that splinter of
salt, blood, chance
as she walks back into
her life, puts on
the detritus of rubber
sneakers, car keys, mouth
for smiling and eating and
making clever remarks. Other
women will sometimes look
too deeply into each
other's eyes and know
too much, feel themselves
slip, before their hands rise
to their faces and press it all
back into place.

My Niece Dreams

she lives in a lighthouse. She must put on
a huge yellow slicker and whaler's hat
to tend the light at 3 a.m.

She grew up as I did
in the land-locked Midwest,
no sailor's daughter, though her father yearns
for a sea-life even he cannot
quite imagine as he sings Jimmy Buffet
and drives the swells of Wisconsin.

Recently heartbroken, a girl who believes
in Fiestaware and teaching the poor,
this oldest sister, peacemaker, smiles

even when the house dims and threatens. She knows
what she is doing, up there in the tower.
She is trying to make the passage safe

for her brother and sister. Behind her ribs
in that salty world, she opens a door
and climbs the spiral stairs. When she gets

to the top, maybe she will open
her mouth and say something her whole
family has been waiting to hear
for generations, her voice

a light strong enough
to blind us all.

The Revilers

In the medicine cabinet the bottle is turned
so in an angled glance she reads "Rain Reviler."
It is the title of some little-known job
in the government, a position
filled only by the austere of this world.
The Rain Reviler takes over all the complaining
for everyone in Washington, D.C. when it rains,
grumbling about wet socks, the smell of wool,
defective windshield wipers, running ink
and umbrellas blowing inside-out like flowers—
leaving the elite free for their own special perversions.

It is a good idea. If one person were designated
official reviler of something we all take time
out of our busy schedules to curse,
imagine the savings in money, effort, and emotion.
The school bus painters could go on
as if in a dream, a perfect dream with
not only orange-yellow school buses but
yellow trees, and sidewalks, and fences,
and children. The poets could rhapsodize without
interruption, the makers of MSG could go about their business
with blithe spirits, spontaneous combustion
could go on atavistically, taunting science.

When she touches the bottle, it falls to the floor
with a brittle crack. Its false name rolls
and coalesces as "Pain Reliever";
she is looking for the answer to pain
in the wrong form. That kind of pap

will not numb her. She opens the door
on a reluctant outer world and steps across,
into the silk sheets of water,
into the dark but auburn afternoon.

Poetry Prompt

How would you like to die? I ask my student,
both of us raw with the torn-away-mother-wound, both hard
flat surfaces for light to bounce off, both without
any clever answers. *What would you*

choose? And, of course, I'm imagining
what I'd choose: the various scenarios of surprise
or foreknowledge, who I'd kiss

if I knew I were dying in a month, what earthy
chocolate confections I'd devour in my last week if
my heart were going to stop anyway. I wish
I could believe I'd be happy
enough that a sudden exit would be no real

interruption. But, as always, I'm paralyzed
with doubt and the sense of everything
left undone—I'm still that girl sleepwalking
out to feed the horses at midnight, bare feet and nightgown
making trails in the snow.

My mother had six months, and her youngest
nearing forty. My student looks at everything
in my office but me with 22-year-old eyes

and won't sit down. I think
her mother left so much unfinished,
even as I watch this daughter

gather her books like the pieces
of a quilt, like the jumbled sea-pebbles of a poem,

and take up a sharp
tool to cut and piece together
what she must, her life's pattern
growing under her hands,
line by wrenching line.

Metropolitan

I still don't believe I have traveled four times to this city
whose subways and crime were offered up
all through my childhood as the bogeyman, my bones
quivering at the sound of its very name.
I know what I am: a woman
held together with bailing twine and paint,

peeling and weathered like old barns or the paintings
I have come to see at the biggest museum in this city.
My husband leads me through the Spanish modernists, distorted women's
bodies and parts, floating triangles and hands reaching up
towards a skyless frame. I whisper alternate names
for these works of art: "Viewer as Prey," "Boiled Bones

Constructed of Fava Beans." It is small-minded, but my bones
ache with a flu I carried south on the train, and these paintings
leave me queasy. It is so much easier to name
what alienates than what transports. I want to blame the city
with its fancy words for north and south: uptown
and downtown, lingo I think only a woman

in heels can say naturally, the kind of woman
I fear would judge me and find me wanting, not bony
enough or chic enough or up
on the latest anything. So I drag my husband toward paintings
and tapestries that graced some rich medieval city,
happy among saints and beasts with names

I once knew, or could know if I wanted. History is about naming
and naming pleases me, as does the woman's
cross that unexpectedly tightens my throat, its gold filigree a city

of interlocking shapes like perfect rib bones
protecting the secret inside. No sweep of paint
holds me so enthralled. And then we step up

into ordinary light, the great room's ceiling so far up
it seems mythical. We say each other's names
as if to establish that we are flesh, not paint.
I point to a young woman
on a bench, her eyes half-lidded, the bones
of her face as strong as this city.

"Look," I say. "She is art." My husband looks up at a woman standing
on the stairs behind us. "Her, too?" Yes. Her unknown name, her bones
under the seams of her red coat. If I could, I'd paint the city inside us all.

Return

In one dream I've returned
to my childhood home
and something is jarringly different—
the roof is slanting glass, or the yard is a river—
but there are always horses;

and in another I'm sent back
to high school, to make up those classes
that, untaken, invalidate all my education since.
In both I doggedly test their reality,
convinced *This is a dream...
ridiculous... impossible...*

But sometimes I wake thinking
I've got to feed the horses
and I see a girl,
bare feet burning in the snow,
walking in her sleep towards a quiet barn,
hair behind her like a flag in the dark,

and I wonder if she will ever do
what she has left so long undone.

V

In XOXOXO,
For example, Miss, which are the hugs
And which the kisses? Does anybody know?
I could argue either way: the O's
Are circles of embrace, the X is someone
Else's star burning inside your mouth;
Unless the O is a mouth that cannot speak,
Because, you know, it's busy.

—James Galvin, from "Dear Miss Emily"

Here, Where I Carry My Blessings

Inside my right wrist
I have had since I can remember—all
my life, probably—
a half-inch wide and two inches long
faintly purple-green convexity
with the same veins
running through it as run through my left
wrist, flat as anyone's. Perhaps

I am storing the seeds of my future self
in that soft extra flesh. Perhaps in my last extremity,
desperate, I could tear open that little pouch
with my teeth and find the sustenance I need. Or maybe
if that packet is ruptured, the alien DNA will flood
my system and I'll be instantly
transformed. Maybe if cut there
I will bleed green ooze. Or I'm invulnerable
to arrows except if they hit just that spot.
Or, if kissed, that wrist would sprout
the world tree. I could be carrying
secrets we will need in ten years. I could be
far older than I seem, have direct
communication with the Ancient of Days but
no idea how to use it. I could be a vampire's
wet dream, the chosen blood. Come,

touch me here, where I am
not normal. I want
to see what miracles might happen.

Opium Summer

Summer is the season of sex
and convertibles, big humid
skies and sun that makes you just want
to lie down in your skin. Breathing
becomes a task requiring both concentration
and resolve; there is never quite enough breath left
for laughter, for example, unless you practice,
like a swimmer or a singer. And you want to
sing, your voice like a flashlight pointing up
at the stars. You want ice
and winged insects, the sweetness of the little blonde
boy who held your hand when you were six.

Inside the house the grownups are
talking, talking, while you slip off
with your adolescent body,
sloughing twenty-some years
to hang out under the trees
in a dark you never got tired of but somehow
were supposed to outgrow. Anything

might happen in the summer, at night, under the heavy
sighs of beasts too big to see. You might
go to sleep beside their lumbering bodies
and dream of wandering the wide world

atop a great furry back,
desert streaming away beneath you, with all
the gardens of the ancient world
rising like magic before your eyes. You might
never want to wake up.

Elaine Dreaming

A professor is one who talks in someone else's sleep.

—*W. H. Auden*

My student tells me the dream she had
between classes on a Tuesday afternoon:
she is surrounded by men with no hands,
at a bar, dancing. There is never enough
dancing in my dreams—quotidian things, really, my mother
saying *That's stupid* and hanging up, rain
turning earth to mud under my desperate feet
as dogs wander too close to the road.
I think there should be a dial-up dream hotline
we can call if ours aren't interesting enough
and to talk shop beyond Freud & Jung. If a tiger smells like spring
in mine, will the flowers survive tonight's frost?
When you have that one where the ringing sends you
searching for the goddamn
phone, and you're pulling and pulling on a drawer
from which the sound issues like steam, and finally
you get it open and wake up
and your lover tells you no, the phone never rang, the alarm
was obediently quiet, the whole house, in fact, conspired in silence
to allow you a peaceful nap—well, what should you make
of that?
        Because after the men with no hands got her drunk
and she passed out, I entered my student's dream, insisting
she get out her poetry and have something
to say about it. From the pit of her subconscious
to this poem to mine isn't much of a jump, so when those men
show up and start waving their stumps
while a little ass-shaking music plays

in my kitchen, I want to know what they mean—
whether to push them out into the late April sunshine
or take off my hands and feel
that heavenly helplessness right along with them,
let whatever's baking burn itself down
while we dance and dance like the happy dead.

Hoping to Learn from Wilbur, Who Said Love Calls
Us to the Things of This World

In the quiet between
passing cars I hear a woodpecker
hammering for insects; the thump of a horse
searching his bucket for the last
mouthful of grain; a moorhen's muted
trumpet of disgruntlement from a nearby pond;
a small dog barking
through his sliding glass doors
at me, walking in this Florida spring dusk
that feels like deep summer in my native
Illinois. I am thinking of ways

we see love in the world,
how you said we all fail every day
to love each other enough, and if we just could
then this world would be paradise. How

I said you had it backwards, that most
of us don't love ourselves
enough, we walk around stung
by self-judgment that blinds us,
we carry burdens as heavy as they are
invisible.

I don't know. Every moment
love leaks from me
like water until I fear my touch
will drown others. I banter
with the pharmacist and he offers
a hug, and we two near-strangers cling

to each other like seeds to a deer's coat,
hoping, perhaps, to be taken
to some earth where we can sprout.

On the way back to my house
I pick a white clover,
and the scent of Illinois curls
around me; I can almost
feel a soft, sweet hand brushing my hair
back from my face. I don't believe

love can solve everything. Love pulls me painfully
back through the years and the miles to when
I first knew myself, the only time I knew
myself to be part of the sky and the trees
and the long grass beside our gravel driveway.

Somehow I think you
have more hope than I do. But I am trying
to walk into this world, while the songs
of cicadas fall around me like stars.

I Want

a dark path through a creaking wood, owls
calling from every corner, antlers, blood, a wolf's speed,
a distant bell, tangles of honeysuckle, gusts
of stars, space to expand to dragon size,
orange sunsets full of lust, night and more
night (cold, sharp, humid as breath),
papery leaves, horses, more than I deserve, paradoxes,
cold water, soft
grass, what I left behind
in the barn when I was ten and had to move away,
those stubborn barnacles of chance and serendipity
that gradually sloughed off me through adolescence,
a way out of the tunnels, a way into the sky,
hooves to run on, to understand
your eyes at last.

Waiting on the Sky

The house is falling delicately
nose-first into the ready earth,
fault lines appearing in the ceiling, and we
go about our usual business
drinking tea and collecting mosses and beads
for decoration. Outside
the coyotes are calling, throwing up their heads
to nip at the wind, bleeding into the trees
like we all bleed, going
back into the dark. Tell me

how your fingers touch
the sheets, pulling
them up to your chin when what you want
is to crush the fabric in your fists.
Tell me closed eyes and the body's
longing, how being known is not enough,
how nothing is—not even kisses—
not when all of you
is a mouth hungry for angels
and you are so afraid
they are not for you; they are
for you but not in this world; they don't
exist; they do.

The Observable Universe

I want to say I have a star
inside, not some twinkly animated sweet
thing but a big, pulsing
ball of plasma so bright it's going
to cut holes in my skin one of these days
just to let the light out. And I don't know
what'll happen after that—
maybe everyone I know will turn inside-
out and we'll play at making
constellations in the dark where we live. I'm a little
afraid of that star burning
steadily at my rib cage like possibilities,
like those moments in childhood when you believe
your life is going to add up to
something more. But I'm just as afraid
some day I'll open the door of my sternum
and find behind it only
ordinary black space, the pinpricks
of white so far away I might look
at them in wonder but never in a whole lifetime
ever reach them, not even
if I started traveling right now.

Katie-Less

In a world without me, hundreds—no,
thousands—of people would have one less crush
in their lives. My friends
would have a name melting
in the back of their minds like a sugar cube,
a name they'd never learned but knew
despite logic. In a world without
me, stars would retreat
a short distance, considering their places
again; grass would stand watching
the road for something
to happen; trees would take
deep breaths and remain stoic.
Everything I love would be less
loved—and wouldn't that
be a shame? Sometimes I think about
being a horse in a blue pasture, a hawk crying
my heart out to the wind. But I wouldn't be
anything in a world without me, even less
than the first sweet molecules of hydrogen and oxygen
to touch your lips
when you tilt a glass of water back
to slake your thirst.

Apple, Word, Kiss

It is for this
I was made: to be in love
with a multitude of faces, to feel laughter
like a finger run lightly
across the skin inside my elbow,
to roll in gardenias like a dog, to sing
with hands and teeth and nape,
to murmur confidences into the ears
of animals, to circle boys
with my arms and notice
eyelashes staining girls' cheeks,
to speak and to swallow, to kiss and to beg
to be kissed, my mouth
a bird leaping
from the top of a tall pine, and the air—
love—its inevitable medium, silky
and fundamental as words.

Acknowledgments

Grateful acknowledgement is made to the following publications in which these poems appeared, sometimes in different forms:

Blood Lotus: "Elaine Dreaming"
Conte: "Years Like Rows of Corn"
The Examined Life: "Here, Where I Carry My Blessings," "Ten Weeks In"
Eye Socket Journal: "Katie-Less"
The Flying Island: "Return"
The Gettysburg Review: "Even in the Pretend World (There is Longing)"
Hobble Creek Review: "The Uncertainty Principle"
Jabberwock Review: "Apple, Word, Kiss," "Ode to Gardenias"
Jane's Stories IV: Bridges and Borders: "Manifesto"
Louisiana Literature: "Need: A Sestina"
Poetry Kanto: "Creation," "Hydra"
The River King Poetry Supplement: "The Revilers," "The Siren Song of
    Corn Country"
Sou'wester: "Metropolitan"
South Dakota Review: "Boys," "Hoping to Learn from Wilbur, Who Said
    Love Calls Us to the Things of This World"
Terrain.org: "Chimes"
Valparaiso Poetry Review: "Some River"

Endless thanks to Michael Hettich, who not only read and improved all the poems in this book and shaped the manuscript itself, but also (gently) demanded I write every week and continually inspired me with his own beautiful poetry. This book would not exist without you, Michael.

So much gratitude also for the support and community of my students and former students, as well as the welcoming literary community in Florida, most notably the talented and warm-hearted Gianna Russo, who also honed many of these poems with her insightful comments.

For general wonderfulness and life-giving, loving wisdom, I'd like to thank all my friends and loved ones, particularly Dorey Riegel, Carolyn Alessio, Geoff Schmidt, Jon Chopan, Liz Kicak, and the incomparable, incandescent Ira Sukrungruang.

Much editing and revising—with the astute help of Lee Passarella of FutureCycle Press—was done during a residency at the Atlantic Center for the Arts, and I'm very grateful for the support and time at this unique organization.

Cover art by Carol Beck; author photo by the author; cover and interior book design by Diane Kistner (dkistner@futurecycle.org); Adobe Garamond text and titling

About FutureCycle Press

FutureCycle Press is dedicated to publishing lasting English-language poetry and flash fiction books, chapbooks, and anthologies in both print-on-demand and ebook formats. Founded in 2007 by long-time independent editor/publishers and partners Diane Kistner and Robert S. King, the press incorporated as a nonprofit in 2012. A number of our editors are distinguished poets and authors in their own right, and we have been actively involved in the small press movement going back to the early seventies.

The FutureCycle Poetry Book Prize and honorarium is awarded annually for the best full-length volume of poetry we publish in a calendar year. Introduced in 2013, our Good Works projects are devoted to issues of global significance, with all proceeds donated to a related worthy cause. We are dedicated to giving all authors we publish the care their work deserves, making our catalog of titles the most distinguished it can be, and paying forward any earnings to fund more great books.

We've learned a few things about independent publishing over the years. We've also evolved a unique, resilient publishing model that allows us to focus mainly on vetting and preserving for posterity the most books of exceptional quality without becoming overwhelmed with bookkeeping and mailing, fundraising activities, or taxing editorial and production "bubbles." To find out more about what we are doing, come see us at www.futurecycle.org.

www.ingramcontent.com/pod-product-compliance
Lightning Source LLC
Chambersburg PA
CBHW070007100426
42741CB00012B/3147